Plate Spinning
and
Hoop Jumping

A Journey Through Home Education

A Warwickshire Mum

Chapter 1

Lots of people have asked me over the years how have I home educated my children? I've chatted a bit with them about what I've done, but somehow it seemed wrong, as it's more about what the children have done and not about me.

I was asked if I could write a book about, "How to home educate." But I didn't think I could, or should, for that would suggest that there is a right way to home educate and that I know the formula.

Years have passed and again the question and requests of "How did you do it and still get your children to university?" It was them; I just facilitated a love of learning.

Then the covid 19 pandemic hit, and I was again asked repeatedly for advice on how to home educate, from desperate parents who overnight had to become their children's teachers. I still had reservations about writing a book, although I would speak to parents on the phone.

So, how come you are reading a book about "How?", well it was put to me by someone younger and much wiser, that a cook writes a recipe book, then the reader will use it, adapt it, adjust it and create recipes based on the original cook's ideas. So that's how I view this book, it's not a set of rules, or even a recipe, it's a set of examples that worked for my family. This is not a "do it my way guide", but more a, "I did it my way account." There will be things you disagree with, things you may try, then reject or things that you decide to try, then adapt to suit your family.

Home education is a journey, a voyage of discovery, a chance to explore rather than blindly accept facts, a way to find understanding, rather than learn parrot fashion.

My daughter spent two years at a further education college and one night exploded,
"I love learning, I loathe education."

To me this summed up everything I've done, it was always what I'd hoped, to raise children who had a love of learning. Children who were open to asking questions and explore things for themselves. To me this is education.

Education that is just a passive set of hoops to jump through, is not true education, but a suffocating time-consuming existence that needs to be got through to tick the boxes of 'an education' as marked by whatever government is in power.

To confuse compulsory schooling with equal educational opportunity is like confusing organised religion with spirituality. One does not necessarily lead to the other.

Schooling confuses teaching with learning, grade advancement with education, a diploma with competence, and fluency with the ability to say something new.

Wendy Priensnitz

Chapter 2

It would be helpful, I think, to give you some background to how we came to be a home educating family. This decision will be as diverse as the families who choose this path. There is no 'type' of family who home educate, it is a very diverse community. Often people think we must have been teachers to be involved in providing our children's education, that's not the case. This wasn't the case for us, so I think I should give you a little bit of our history and how we became home educators.

It all began last century; I had trained as a nursery nurse after a non-descript time at school. I neither loved it or hated it, I just went, tried, tried some more and didn't do very well. I was discouraged from asking questions and found it all dull and disconnected from real life and I couldn't see how it would benefit me in life.

As a qualified nursery nurse, I went off to work as a Nanny for lots of different families. Via these families I came into contact with some of the best private schools this country had to offer. I collected and dropped off at Steiner playgroups, Montessori prep schools and choir schools, as well as ferrying children to music, sports clubs and tutor groups.

After a few years of being a private nanny I started work in a state-run nursery school and saw education from another angle. Staff, students, national curriculum and Ofsted. It was working in that environment with those children that I felt the first concerns with organised education. It felt restrictive and narrow, but it was a happy place, and it prepared the children well for the formal setting of school.

As I observed the children and made the notes on their progress and ticked boxes as to what each child had done each day, I began to question how learning could be broken down into tick boxes. Who were we ticking boxes for? I could see no benefit for the children. What did the children gain from sitting cross legged on the carpet while I held up a story book? Surely a child was more engaged with the story when leaning against my knee, seeing me really read and drinking in the pictures and associating the page turning with the words, translating the strange shapes of letters with words, making connections for themselves without being 'taught'.

Questions surfaced and I listened to the replies from the teaching staff of the school the nursery was attached to. I spent some time supporting in the classrooms higher up the school and saw how lessons were planned and delivered. I also listened to the responses of the children as I stood on playground duty. More questions, to which I did not receive answers, other than, 'children need to be here.'

I then became pregnant and while on maternity leave, I found a book in the local library, on the parenting shelf about home education. Sitting there like a beached whale I started to read it. I liked the idea, it addressed so many of the questions I had asked about formal education. But I thought surely this wasn't legal or allowed these days and certainly wouldn't be possible for ordinary semi-detached dwelling families.

Life continued, I did not return to work after maternity leave, but started to childmind. Our son was joined by a daughter and before long we were looking at playgroups for our son. We settled him in, and we had his name down for a good local school. We even ordered the name tapes; the well-ordered path and predictable journey was all mapped out.

I loved those preschool years. I loved sharing time and the wonder of the world through the eyes of a small boy and girl. It was a great time. Life was slow and full. We stopped on walks and learnt letters from local street signs, tracing our fingers over the shapes of the letters. We learnt to spell 'wait' from the red man on the road crossing signs. We looked at everything, talked, questioned and explored. Even household tasks took on a new interest as we paired socks and counted them in twos, or talked about germs as we washed our hands.

These were happy years, enjoying life from a child's viewpoint and visiting the library, museum, toddler group and park and introducing them to life.

We splashed in puddles, wrote in condensation on the kitchen windows, we baked, read, made stuff, gardened and had fun. One day we spent ages stood out on the front path, as our son had noticed that house 2 was next to house 4, who had stolen house 3? He looked and discovered that it was on the other side of the road. This led to a walk back and forth across the road looking at house numbers, with road safety thrown in for good measure. We talked about the sequence of numbers, the phrase 'odd and even numbers' and how, odd numbers were on one side, even numbers on the other. The question was asked 'what makes a number odd?' so home we went and aided by a bag of dolly mixture sweets we addressed odd and even numbers. We divided the sweets by the two children and showed how the odd numbers could not be divided equally. Our son was four and could now work with numbers 1-12, he could also add, take away and divide.

Then came the day of the new parents' welcome evening. I went, I listened, I wanted to be sick!

We had chosen this school because they had a policy of two reception classes of twenty-five children and this small introductory class size was something we really liked. At that parents evening on that hot June evening we were told that due to a reduced number of applicants that year, they would not be able to fund the two classes, but instead have one class of forty children.

My four year would be in a class of forty! Moment of parental panic.

40 children, 1 teacher and 1 teaching assistant. How much attention could each child get? I thought of the 1000's of questions that we would try to answer each day, no teacher could tackle those x40. To make myself feel better after the formal talk I queued to speak to the class teacher.

"My son can read; how will you be able to manage with him in a class where you might have some children who come from a background where they perhaps haven't had access to books?"

"We have plenty of library books, he can read those while the rest catch up." Was her reply.

Yes, the library was well stocked and a lovely environment. BUT alarms rang in my head, red flags danced before my eyes. If he waited for the rest to catch up how could he be learning? I thought again of the 1000's of questions we answered each day, I worried, no, I panicked. How could that poor teacher cope and meet the needs of all 40 children? What was education if you had to stand still to allow others to catch up with you?

That night was long as my husband and I talked around the problem. We number crunched, could we go private? No. Next morning I phoned round other schools that were local (ish), but found no other vacancies. Panic.

Exhausted and frightened about the looming spectre of September and school, I bumped into a friend who owned a playgroup. She asked what was wrong and after I had explained she just smiled and said, "You could home educate."

I remembered the book from the library and suddenly felt relieved, excited and less tired. Life could continue as it was, learning through life. But could I do it?

My friend knew of a family who had come to her playgroup and then gone on to home educate their children. She put us in touch.

Within three days I'd met with three families who all home educated their children. They answered my questions and let me talk through my worries. They explained what they did and how. These three families all approached their home education in vastly different ways. One family did school at home in a very structured way, one the total opposite with autonomous education. They loaned me some books and details of Education Otherwise and HEAS, (Home Education Advisory Service) and the contact details of local home education groups. Suddenly September ceased to be so scary, there were options, we didn't have to send our son to school.

Playgroup had prepared the children to move onto 'big' school, so once we had made our choice, we discussed it with our son. After all, it was, he who was the reason for this change from 'normal' behaviour. He agreed, so in June 1999 we walked together to deliver the letter to the school saying we no longer required the place for that September.

We were home schoolers. We were outside the system and free to make our own choices as a family as to how and what we would learn. Life could carry on as it had since the children had arrived. We could carry on learning from one another, about one another and about the wider world in which we lived.

In the county we lived in at that time there were about 24 home educating families and we quickly joined them and met up for monthly meetings and trips. Only 24 other families, it was like a family in itself, and that left a large number of people who we knew who didn't know anything about home education.
"Was it legal?"
"What about socialisation?"
"How could we possibly do exams?"
 He was four for goodness sake!

Some people would support us, some were going to walk away from us, some asked some interesting questions, and some were to stay with us for our whole journey. Some people were quite hostile, and some were doubters of the whole process. I asked one doubter what it was she feared that I could not provide for our children that a school did, what exactly did she think our children would miss out on? Her reply, "They will never learn to put up their hand or stand in a queue."

As seriously as I could manage, I replied, "We would always look out for the longest queue in the supermarket so they can gain first-hand experience of how to queue."

If the ability to queue was the worst thing they would miss out on by not going to school, then I was not too concerned. No one had suggested anything that made me feel that I needed to send my children to school, but what it did do was make me stop and think. I thought a lot about schools and education.

Do you need to go to school to become an educated person? No, was the simple answer. History is full of non-schooled people who have gone on to make amazing discoveries in science and medicine, music and the arts. School and education are two separate things which in our society have become interlinked, but in my mind, they are two different things and to become educated you don't need to go to school.

Every now and then in the home education journey we undertook there would be times when I had doubts and worries. When these times happened, I always came back to this, school is only one way to gain an education - you don't need school to become educated. For us, I knew it was the right choice.

There is no school
Equal to a decent
Home, and no teacher
Equal to a virtuous parent.

Mahatma Gandhi

Queue here

Chapter 3

September 1999

So, it began. A new term of a new academic year. Little children carrying bright lunch boxes walked past our house. It was real, we had done it, we had set off on our own journey. We had membership to Education Otherwise, we had books on the shelf all about education; Steiner, Montessori, Charlotte Mason and John Holt. We were home educators, but what now?

We decided that for us the best approach would be to start each day with a little 'formal' work. Daddy had to go to work, so as he left, we would sit down for our work.

Around a low table we would all sit and spend a little time with maths and English. This might be playing with dice, dividing Lego bricks, turning the hands-on paper plate clocks we had made, or counting coins and looking at their values. Sometimes we would do simple work sheets and written sums.

Our English we approached in a huge variety of ways, usually through exploring a topic. I would start by reading a story or something from a magazine. This would either be something that had sprung from a child's question, or something I knew they would find interesting, springing from their interests. We would then do a little writing, starting first with me scribing for them, then as they grew more independent with writing they would write as much or as little as they wanted. We created lots of little books on all kinds of topics.

Some fun books we made were based on words from the same family of spelling, for example cook, book, look. We used a hole punch to make the 'oo' and added the letters before and after. Then we illustrated silly stories about cooks who put books on hooks and looks at the fish.

These books we shared with family and friends and enjoyed our first adventures as authors, or explorers of new ideas and places.

A lot of what we learnt came from the children's questions. I quickly noticed that by answering a question the children asked, they retained the information that they were given, if I tried to teach, they forgot.

I had to learn to listen and pick up on their questions and from there we would explore a topic.

"Why is Warwickshire called 'Shakespeare county'?"

"Why do I poo?"

"Why do the windows go steamy when we cook pasta, and where does pasta come from?"

We might have only done schoolwork for ½ -1 hour a morning, but our exploring went on all day.

People generously gave us books and 'school' type resources. But as we gradually relaxed into what we were doing, I discovered we were just using a good children's atlas and an illustrated children's encyclopaedia. These took us on journeys around the world. But our main starting point were lots and lots of good children's stories.

We curled up for hours and visited Narnia, travelled the Oregon trail, hid from the Nazis and sat under the table clutching our gas mask boxes as we read about children in the Blitz. We joined children of different cultures and different periods of history. We dressed up as Egyptians and Romans, made props then held an appropriate feast.

Learning was much bigger than sitting pen in hand, writing. Our trips to the supermarket would take ages as we weighed fruit and veg, looked for cereal with the lowest salt and sugar content and talked about best price per hundred grams. We talked about where our food came from, how it might have travelled here and how we would store it and how we might eat it.

Over the veg counter we practiced our basic French, asking each other where apples, bananas or oranges were. Then we would count them into bags. In the queue we would estimate the cost of our shopping. Life skills were absorbed, not taught and set the children up for life.

In fact, those life skills have been really useful. When our son and then daughter went off to university, they spent the first terms helping other freshers learn to budget, shop sensibly and cook. They weren't mixing with daft people; these were clever kids who had entered university but had missed out on the day to day skills for life. Our daughter's sewing skills were in great demand, sewing on buttons and turning up trouser legs for some of the university nursing students.

Life was our children's school room. We are lucky in this country to have a rich source of places to visit. Museums, libraries, galleries, farm parks, country parks, historical sites, the list goes on. Most of these places had 'What's on' events lists, so we would look and see what was available. Some were specifically for children in school holidays, others were open to all. Some were free, some charged a nominal fee, some were expensive. We would sort through and see what inspired us the most. We explored, listened and learnt. I also say we, as I learnt so much alongside the children.

Most of all, learning was inspired by seeing people engaged in their daily tasks who we chatted to and were willing to share their knowledge and show us their skills.

There was the man from the fire service painting hydrant covers who explained why he was doing it, how hoses would be attached, then let the children each paint one.

One day in the coffee shop attached to our Parish Church we saw a small door in the wall open. We asked where the door led and were shown the stairs inside the tower. We were then given a guided tour of the tower and shown where the bells were hung and told all about the bell ringers. Yes, we were allowed a go at ringing the bells.

We joined community projects to make hanging baskets. We discovered how to make cheese and pasta. We talked, watched and explored. We kept diaries of our adventures; it gave us a reason to write. We drew pictures of what we had done and took photographs and added these to our diaries. It gave us a lovely record of our journey.

Learning never stopped. Even when our son ended up in hospital, some of the parents whose children shared the ward had the added stress that their children were missing school, that was one less thing for us to be concerned by.

Hospital became school, x rays were exciting question starters. Bones and joints intriguing. We bought a plastic skeleton so that he could 'see' what was inside. The staff were lovely and because we took an interest took time to explain and show our son details of his insides.

Through everything, learning never stopped. We continued the daily 'schoolwork', sitting down pen in hand as Daddy went to work. The discipline, routine and order of work set up each day before we stood up and got on with the real learning.

I tried to create different learning zones in the house, in the corner of the kitchen I put a small plastic chest of drawers, the top only about a foot square. On this was our explorers' tray, I bought some cheap plastic kits of a human heart, a plastic jaw and teeth, a skeleton and these took turns on the tray along with a plug and screwdrivers. Accompanying these objects were a magnifying glass, ruler, pens and paper, and a simple book about the objects. They were just there waiting for enquiring minds and exploring fingers.

Baskets of books were left accessible and rotated on a regular basis. Both fact and fiction. Pictures and posters decorated the dining room walls, some bought, many home-made. These were all great ways to stimulate questions and open enquiring minds.

Our windowsills housed science projects, and we raised seeds and plants. We measured our runner beans' growth and kept a record, drawing pictures of them before planting them out in the garden.

We made and flew paper aeroplanes, measured the distance they flew and read about the Wright brothers. We had fun.

The family grew. Big son and daughter came along to the antenatal checks and listened to the baby's heartbeat. Having mixed with a wide range of people of all ages, through home education groups and family friends, they were confident around babies and ready to take on the job of big brother and sister, to a new brother in December 2000.

A new millennium, a new century and three children together at home. It was wonderful, as they learnt from one another. The needs of a baby then a toddler were understood because we were together all the time, not separated into peer groups.

One of the biggest joys of home education has been that there is no age barrier to friendships. By being at home and part of the community, the children have not been segregated to their own age group. They have learnt by observation the needs of the little ones, but also the elderly and unwell. They don't fear disability or infirmity as they have seen it first-hand. Life is full of people of all ages and abilities and my children have been part of that great family, and through it have never been worried by difference.

Socialisation has always been a word brought up when people asked about home education. In fact, it has always surprised me how often this was flagged up as a possible downside to home ed. No one worries about a school child's socialisation, but they could possibly mix with no-one, be lonely and isolated, then go home to an empty house to spend hours watching TV or playing on a games machine before going to bed.

One child who came to our home ed group, had endured school for a few years, being bullied and speaking to no-one all day. The staff never noticed, they thought she was a 'good' girl, quiet and conscientious. She was so lonely and unhappy, the school day was torture. In only a few weeks this silent, sad child was laughing happily with friends.

Socialization for us as home educators was and is wide and varied, just different to a school child.

The children joined Cubs and Rainbows, then Brownies. They were members of the church choir. Together and individually they have taken part in sports clubs; kayaking, cricket, swimming, rock wall climbing, fencing, archery and athletics. Some of these were taster sessions, some school holiday summer clubs, some taken up and done over years. Two children went on to become karate blackbelts, one took a qualification to coach kayaking.

Through being part of a church the children joined in plays, took part in reading at services and then Big son went on to learn how to operate the sound desk - a skill he took forward into university, where he found himself in constant demand by societies to run sound and lighting for events.

As the children grew older, friendships have deepened and become stronger, not because friends have been seen daily, but because friends have been kept in touch with and friendships nurtured.

Socialisation is the ability to communicate in all kinds of situations and to know and understand the codes of conduct in different environments. The confines of the school room with only peer directed behaviours doesn't provide a child with an idea of how to behave in different places. Schools get round this by using role play - we played for real. By accompanying me to the bank or hospital or to see a bereaved neighbour they saw and learned the way to behave.

Having close contact with a range of different adults, the children had role models and always someone around to answer questions and help explain the mysteries of the world around them. They also saw that adults don't necessarily have all the answers, but they too needed to research and look up an answer.

Coming back from a day trip we saw a drunk behaving erratically, so we talked about alcohol abuse and substance abuse. The seeing of life up close has meant it has been real and relevant, rather than just another lesson to be learnt.

Socialization has been different, at age 10 Big son listed amongst his friends a gentleman in his 80's and a 6-month-old baby. Relationships have developed and eye contact encouraged, providing skills for real life.

I know I'm about to generalise, but usually if you speak to a home educated young person, they will speak to you treating you as an equal and entering conversation.

Just an interesting observation, which I think comes from socialising across the spectrum of ages and having everything discussed rather than peer responses, that when we had a postcard on our wall of Michael Angelo's 'David' and home educated children came in and saw it, their response was;

"Who carved it?"

"Talented sculpture."

"You can see all his muscles."

When school children visited there was giggling and their response - embarrassed giggling,

"Look, he's got no clothes on."

Educating the mind without educating the heart
is no education at all.

Aristotle

Chapter 4

"But how?"
"How do you teach?"
"How do you know what to teach?"

These common questions followed me through all the years of home education. In 2020, with home education forced upon families by the covid crisis, some schools are providing work, or work outlines for families to follow. That is not how home education works for the majority of families, some do school at home, but most don't.

How and why? These were my main starting questions in all we did.

There is a huge industry of education. There are so many curriculums, reading schemes, workbooks, games and equipment that we are seduced by. Then there are schools touting for your child, flouting their best bits, encouraging you that this place is the best place for your child. Then of course there are the teachers - highly qualified individuals, knowledgeable and experienced to teach and guide your child. How could I replace all this? How could I teach?

Cue, moments of panic and self-doubt. Mug of tea, think it through, I knew why I wanted to do this. Now to sort out the "how do I teach?"

So, this is what I did. I started out by looking at different school curriculum. It was easy to find as most schools had it printed in their prospectus. I collected them from all my local schools, both state and private, and spread them out. I compared them all, looking at what they each considered a child should be studying. Here I found my first discrepancy, that despite a national curriculum, different places put different emphasis on different things. So I questioned why we teach what we do in schools. Why are Tudors more important than Victorians or vice versa? Why do some places look at Egyptians instead of Romans?

After reading and researching, we chose to set our education in our local area to start with. We set off to explore the local museums. We wandered through millennia of local history. The only evidence of our visit and learning, photographs of us dressing up in costumes, stuck in a scrap book about the visit.

We tried to follow up visits with a story that reflected something we had looked at on our visit. One of our local museums had a Victorian school room and kitchen, so the visit was followed up by reading "street child" and "The little princess." We then coloured in pictures of Victorian kitchen maids and wrote about the contrasts of our lives and that of a Victorian child at work.

Sitting in a traffic jam one day on the M40 one of the children read a road sign. "Welcome to Shakespeare's county"
"Why's it called that?"
"We will find out." I replied.
From there we found some abridged children's versions of Shakespeare's plays and read them. We then bought a year pass to the Shakespeare houses and booked to see some of his plays.

Again, we might not have had much evidence of learning. We didn't have pages of 'busy' worksheets, but we had been immersed in the Bard's life and works. We even tried to write a bit of poetry. We used dolls and puppets and put on our plays. We played with words and descriptions. This was History and English learning in action.

One of my best memories was having a picnic in the orchard at Ann Hathaway's cottage and our daughter stood on the picnic table and acted out the role of Juliette in the balcony scene, her brother a reluctant Romeo.

Walks around the local nature reserve had us looking at the information boards and wanting to know more about life cycles, wind power and how the methane gas underground was collected and used to make electricity. Home we would go, to use the wonderful Usborne books, to find out more. We made posters of life cycles and windmills as we looked at wind power, we added a few written notes and put them on the wall for all to admire. Perhaps I'd then challenge them to think of verbs to describe the butterfly's movements and this list would be added to the artwork.

English, science, art all intertwined.

Life provided those early maths lessons as we cooked and weighed and measured. As we shopped, we counted money, added up the cost of two items, found the money needed and worked out the change. These things were not hard to organise, but were time consuming, by going out to shops at quiet times and with time, we could do our maths with life.

I could go on and on about all the activities we did, but you get the picture of the interconnectedness of life-based learning. Doing played a huge part of our life. It is better to experience a river by playing in it than to just study rivers. The other major part of our learning was stories. Stories played a huge part in the early years learning. Stories opened our eyes to other cultures and times. We would hypothesise about a story, how it might end, what a character might do, how would they react, how would we react? But primarily, we read for fun. By me reading to them they could hear words and stories that they could not read, we could talk about meanings of unfamiliar words. We re-read picture books, enjoying the wonderful pictures and flow of language.

If you ask me about what books to read your children, I couldn't answer, as there are so many fantastic children's books. I loved reading the children anything by Shirley Hughes, lingering over the illustrations and really feeling for Alfie when he was locked alone in the house, or working out why his boots felt uncomfortable as he stomped in the puddles and how the problem was prevented from occurring again.

From picture books we progressed to the exciting new worlds of Narnia and travelled on the Hogwarts express to the wizard school with Harry Potter and friends. Old books, new books, all types of genre. Often, I would read a book first to see if I thought it would be of interest to the children. Sometimes topics were in a story that I didn't think they would be ready for, so I might not read it to them, leaving it on the shelf. No book was banned, no topic forbidden, just some were not chosen to be opened.

I could write pages and pages, list after list of books. There are so many and each were read for different reasons. Some families might say no to Enid Blyton, but for me if the 'Magic far-away tree' promotes imagination, play and storytelling, encourages a child to pick up a book and read, then it's a book worth opening.

There are many debates over what children should or should not read, does it matter? If they read and have adults with whom they can discuss the books, then they soon learn to think and make choices about whether or not it is a good story.

Being read to allows a child to develop skills and language without the strain of reading. Following along as a parent reads introduces words and phrases above their reading age and helps them decode the strange shapes that make words.

Comfy cushions, a cosy place, in a tent, under a table or propped against a castle wall, we've read in so many different places. We've taken books everywhere with us and read in many different places, creating family memories. What better way than to connect with the characters than to sit in the museum Anderson shelter and read about the Blitz and World War Two, or under an oak tree our bows and arrows at our feet and reading of the outlaws and Robin Hood.

Books have been a springboard to so much play and exploration. From listening to reading, then inspired to read for themselves. They then began to look out more books by a favourite author and read those for themselves while I continued to read them other things.

"Yeah, yeah, yeah," I hear you say, "learning to read is not that easy or fun."

You may think your child has problems and reading is no fun. But just hold on - I'll address that later, just keep reading, not just this, but also to your children. Being read to is not just for toddlers, listening is a skill to be honed and what better way than sharing a good story together.

Books have also inspired writing. I always had available writing materials, coloured pens and pencils. I made small books of folded paper with funky covers so there was always materials available for any budding author.

Wherever possible I tried to make writing a relevant part of our life. Thank you letters, postcards, notes in the diary, copying out a recipe from a library book to our own recipe book, even writing a shopping list was all writing practice. Most of all it was trying to keep it real and give writing an importance.

For us home education was working, and it was fun. But every now and then I'd have a wobble. Were they learning enough? Would they keep up with their peers if they ever had to go into school? It was then I'd rush into WHSmith's and come out armed with Key Stage books appropriate to their ages.

Usually these workbooks were well received by the children. They liked the stickers or stars and colourful pages. They would start these books with enthusiasm. But after a few days the sameness and repetition would become boring, but they usually raced to get them done. Boxes ticked, parent panic reduced, and we would settle back into our way of doing things; exploring, reading and learning by doing.

We tried to understand events we were going to be involved in. We found out about Guy Fawkes before going to a bonfire party. We were invited to a July 4th party and again tried to find out about that before we went. This was a little bit of a struggle. The local library had nothing; all I could find was a paragraph about those "naughty colonials". This is not something usually covered in English schools. So, I quickly wrote to a friend in America. This resulted in a lovely parcel of books and goodies which told the story of the American's fight for independence.

There were no divisions between life and learning. Even on holiday books came along in the bag, usually something to help me answer questions by a rock pool and probably an exciting story about pirates or smugglers, or a journey on the high seas.

"I suppose it is because nearly all children go to school nowadays and have things arranged for them, that they seem so forlornly unable to produce their own ideas."

Agatha Christie

Chapter 5

To tell or not to tell that is the question…

If you have a child and remove them from school, you must deregister them correctly, otherwise you are allowing your child to truant and are breaking the law. Deregistration is simply a letter sent to your child's head teacher. There are some very good sample letters available online. In fact, I just googled sample letter to deregister child from school U.K. and was surprised by the number of them that popped up.

If you have a child that has never been to school, you are not obliged under current U.K. law to inform your local education authority. This has led to a lot of debate amongst home education families as to whether or not to inform their L.E.A.'s. (Local Education Authority)

There are many good and valid reasons on both sides of this argument. As this is a personal account of our home education, I shall not go into all these debates, but just tell you what we did and why, as it is part of our journey.

Back in the late 1990's, early 2000's there were not many home educating families in our area. It was unusual to see children out and about in school term time. Therefore, as we were a rarity, we made the decision to inform our L.E.A. We had nothing to hide and thought it better to tell them of our choice to home educate, rather than have someone report us for being out of school.

What did this mean to us?

Not much. Each January a lovely lady came to the house and chatted through our educational provision. In the week before we would get out all the previous years' work, sort through it and create a table full of 'stuff' that had been collected and which represented what we had learnt.

I found that the inspections made me notice what we had done. The inspector would always break the work down into traditional school subjects to satisfy her tick box report sheet. This would always worry me. Had we really done geography? Of course, those maps we had made of our journey on holiday and those 3D models we had made of the estuary.

The look back at the work was also quite encouraging, as getting it all out helped us to see the improvements the children had made, especially seeing writing and maths from 12 months ago.

The inspections also made me think of all those academic areas and address them. I am not a musician - switching on a CD is the limit of my skills! I knew that there was a tick box for music, so I addressed this, and we regularly visited local concerts. From organ recitals to brass bands in the local park and our local university's free lunch time concerts. We have listened to and enjoyed a wide range of musical styles and instruments.

Foreign languages were another tick box. My skills definitely don't lie in languages. But I wanted the children to experience them. It wasn't a difficult thing to resolve. We bought some videos in French and some fun language tapes to play in the car.

I also employed a French national student to come for an hour a week to talk and play in French. We talked, we shared food, asked for sweets and ice cream and had fun with the language.

Another family wanted to also learn French, so we joined up. One morning a week we shared kitchen table French fun, it involved a lot of croissants and jam, but we were all talking French. We even made some little French language videos. The children acted, talked and had fun, then we had the video to watch again and again, re-enforcing the language.

We also met another home educating Mum who had been an interpreter for the deaf. It's not a modern foreign language, but it's definitely a modern language and it captured the children's imagination. They loved the lessons. My daughter would use signs to spell out new words and help her remember the spelling. Big son went on to gain a level 1 qualification in British sign language.

The inspector found that a tick box way to measure home education didn't really work and she needed to add additional notes. The reports came back saying that the children were receiving a wide range of educational experiences. The L.E.A were happy, and I was relieved to see that our method of education was working for us.

It's a miracle that curiosity survives formal education.
Albert Einstein

Education is what remains after one has forgotten what one has learned in school.
Albert Einstein

secondary education
grammer school
comprehensive school
private school
academy school
home education

Chapter 6

What next?

The seven years of Big son's primary education passed in a wonderful blur of precious memories. The house became more cluttered with books and toys and the art projects of three children. Our walls hung with pictures they had created, and our windowsills were crammed with science projects.

We knew the local area better than ever. We knew the free museums and places to visit. We knew the walks and where the blue plaques could be found. We knew where to find interesting people, like the traditional book binder tucked away in a side street.

Our circle of friends was more diverse than we could have ever hoped for. We met wonderful people who were willing to share their skills and their culture with us. There was a lovely lady in the post office who always took time and was interested in the children. One day when the post office was quiet, she came out from behind the counter to teach me how to put on a sari.

We began to know our neighbours better and enjoyed one elderly gentleman's stories of being in the merchant navy during the war. He showed us his treasures brought home from his travels.

Then suddenly into this lovely lifestyle came 'secondary school'. Like a Spectre it loomed. It was like dark clouds gathering on the horizon on a sunny day on the beach, which you don't want to end, so try to ignore. Secondary school - it became a major topic of conversation as the eleventh birthday approached.

The local newspaper listed the open days, parents' events and talks by head teachers. I tried to develop an open mind and with the knowledge that I have very few qualifications, not even maths and English (I failed my O'levels in both of these and was diagnosed with dyslexia six weeks before the exams). I set off to explore secondary schools.

"Gulp!"

I toured, I listened, and I questioned. One place I went, I decided no way, over my dead body would he go there. Cramped classrooms of bored-looking teenagers. I knew a new build was about to happen, but the staff would still be the same and those I met no longer seemed to have spark of enthusiasm for their subject. Here, the school day seemed to be no more than a prison sentence for the staff and student to endure and complete.

Then I visited another school. Here I was met with an attitude I liked. Bright corridors, examples of work, and a buzz of enthusiasm. I liked the science labs, the workshops and the head teacher.

Secondary school, yes, it looked good. I knew that Big son would cope with this, even enjoy it. I looked at samples of the year 7's work and thought it didn't look much more advanced than what we were doing. Yes, I decided this was the secondary school for him.

But…

I had not considered Big son's point of view.

He and I set off for the open evening. Together we explored. We went into demonstrations in the science labs and played games in the language labs.

As we went round, I was positive. I had one or two tiny niggles but kept these to myself. I watched Big son take part in everything on offer. We were having a lovely evening.

In each subject area Big son engaged the staff in conversation about their subject. He had a passion for history, in fact he had been a room guide for the National Trust since he was seven. He asked the history teacher what areas they covered in year 7. She replied that they began with local history. He lit up and said, "Wow that's great, isn't it wonderful what we have round here…" he then rattled off famous names connected with our town.

Without moving a muscle in her expression, she looked down at him.

"We don't cover that," she said and turned away.

He turned, a puzzled look on his face, and we left the room. I excused her attitude by saying, "It's getting towards the end of the day. I think people are getting tired."

Then we went into the maths department, Big son loved maths. He beamed as he was offered maths puzzles to do and sat happily at the table.

After completing the activities, he saw a maths problem on the board. Standing square in front of the board he worked his way through each line of the problem. Five minutes later he turned to me and announced the answer.

"Is it right?"

I didn't know. So, he went up to the teacher and asked if he had got it right.

The answer he was given surprised us both. He was told he had got the maths correct, but he shouldn't have done it as it was a GCSE question, and he should not go working outside of his peer group level.

Exit one stunned mother and a shocked eleven-year-old.

All the time we had home educated we had reminded ourselves of the law. "Education must be suitable for a child's age, aptitude and ability, at school or otherwise."

Here we were in a school being told by a teacher that aptitude and ability were unimportant, only age.

I said nothing to the teacher, we just left the maths department. I now had doubts about school. But I couldn't compete at home with the equipment and facilities as well as degree qualified staff in every subject.

Big son was still smiling as we walked back to the car. He enthused about the library, the science activities and the maths work. We got into the car and I handed him the prospectus and application forms to hold.

"You've got so much to tell Daddy about," I said. "Tomorrow we'll fill in these forms and get them sent in."

"I'm not going," he replied.

I sat in the car, open mouthed doing a good impression of a goldfish. "But I thought you liked it?"

"I've had a brilliant evening," he replied, "but Mum, the history teacher didn't like kids. I don't think she even liked her subject. Then there was the maths, I think I'd be bored. If you can't go ahead then how can you learn?"

"But, but, what about socialisation, I can't provide 100 people of your age?"

"Oh Mum! How can you socialise in a school? You're there to listen to the teacher. I'd prefer to have my friends over and spend time with them, rather than a moment while moving to another classroom, or while I'm trying to eat my lunch or go to the loo."

"But, but, but" I stammered. "there are qualified teachers. What about exams?"

"Mum don't worry." He said calmly. "I can look things up and maybe we can save up and I could have a computer. Then it will be even easier to research. I want to stay home educated, and work from home."

Gulp again!

In the face of such maturity and determination, what could I do? Part of our way of life had been respect; respect of someone's opinion, whatever their age. Now here I was torn between the ideas of the world to make my son conform to school, or to continue to respect him as a person, able to make his own choices. He was eleven, I was an adult, what should I do?

We got home and Big son went to bed. Time now to talk without him. We went round and round the subject, round and round and round.

There were only a couple of families locally who had carried home education into secondary education. But these families had wonderful young people, so unlike the stereotype of a teenager. If my children turned out like those young people I would be delighted. But how to do the education and face the exams and challenges of secondary education.

That night we again reassessed what education was. Why do we send children to school? How would we do secondary education? What would we need to change? How could we get qualifications from home? What is the purpose of exams?

Questions went round and round and they then branched out to what are we preparing our young people for? Exams are only a step to further training and work. Why do we work? What is the purpose of work?

Work provides money to live. To live, to be respected, to have life skills, that was my answer. That was what was important. Life skills are as important as exams, in my mind.

Finally, we were getting somewhere. Our son needed to be listened to and be respected. So, he could stay home. He needed to prepare for life. He needed to be prepared for life with not just exams but life skills, so he could live an independent life.

What are life skills? I made a list of what I felt he needed to learn in those secondary years. Personal hygiene, household skills, ironing, laundry and basic sewing, food and nutrition and financial understanding. These things headed my list and have since been proved that they were the right things to put on it.

These invaluable independence skills have held both Big son and daughter in good stead when they headed off to university. They both shared this knowledge and taught their peers in the halls of residence.

As a sign of maturity and instead of going to secondary school we took Big son to the bank and set up a bank account. His small amount of pocket money was paid in monthly and he was given the responsibility to fund a few things. Basic money management, but so important. We also bought him a set of Martin Lewis' money saving expert books which we enjoyed reading with him.

We also began to spend a little more time on formal schoolwork. We bought a science course from an American home school company called 'Sonlight' and we did that daily, not just Big son, but everyone joined in. The science course provide lots of experiments that could be done from home.

School time was now 2-2 ½ hours a day for Big son. That was the only adjustment we made to the start of secondary education years.

Education is
The most
Powerful weapon
Which you can use
To change the world.

Nelson Mandela

Chapter 7

Year 9

Big son suddenly grew taller, as teenage boys do. He was running the sound desk at church for services and helping out with cooking at church lunches, having gained a food hygiene certificate. He continued to volunteer for the National Trust, working once a fortnight as a room steward.

The balanced lifestyle of "schoolwork" and trips to museums, galleries and places of interest had given him a broad idea of what was available in the world after education. He was learning his own strengths and weaknesses. He started to express some ideas of what he might like to do, and he expressed an interest in pursuing a degree in history or maths.

Having an idea of what he might like to do we began to look at options. We looked online and sent off for some university prospectuses. We looked at what qualifications and skills were needed to enter university. We then looked at what A level or post 16 qualifications he would need and what was needed to get onto an A level course.

GCSE's would be the first step to a post 16 qualification. We had four years before GCSE year. Time to just enjoy learning and living.

Of course, this time was not just about Big son, there was our daughter and little son in the mix and their needs to consider and their interests to also meet. They were all different, which was wonderful. Whereas Big son approached everything from a mathematical and science angle, our daughter approached things from an artistic angle and loved literature and language.

Little son was a different character completely. A powerhouse of wriggles and noise. To learn was to move. A pen in hand, with bottom on a seat was agony for him. Upside down, up a tree was the place to discuss times tables or fractions. Bounce about on the trampoline and you could talk about circumference, diameter and other circle geometry. To channel this energy, we went along to a karate class 3 times a week.

I needed to think differently for Little son, the champion wriggler. We did do seated work, but for him it had to have a real purpose. Writing was like getting blood out of a stone...until I bought postcards, to send to friends or grandparents. Real practical tasks that meant something was the way forward with him. That was one of the joys of home education - we didn't need to be confined to a table, a room, a building. We could if we wanted run outside and experience the weather, play in the snow, fly kites in the wind, or make wet footprints and watch them vanish on a warm day.

We read about the Toll Puddle martyrs and the start of trade unions. Then we planned and headed off for a few days holiday to explore the village. We explored the museum and found the graves, then sat under the trees on the village green. We made little scrap books of our trip and discoveries as we sat in the 'bed and breakfast' we stayed in.

Then it happened!

In one week, three people spoke negatively to Big son. Each one saying in one form or another, that maybe this home schooling was o.k. for little ones, they could see he had learnt things, BUT he'd never get qualifications, never go to university, never get a job.

Big son was cross, so was I. I knew that they meant well, those Do Gooders, but they didn't know us, or the thoughts behind our decision. I tried to ignore it. Big son thought about it.

In January he announced he was going to take GCSE's in the summer. He was going to shut up the Do Gooders by passing the exams and passing them early!

Panic from me!

"It's January," I said. "the exams are in May and June."

Big son just shrugged and said, "I'll do it. But no one is to be told."

What a challenge.

What a change.

What a panic (for me).

Cucumber cool, Big son thought about what he would like to try. He thought about what he enjoyed and the things he was good at. He then chose maths because he loved it; Biology because we had done quite a lot of it and it was interesting, Religious studies because as Christians, he thought he ought to know a bit. Then as a fourth he chose Classical civilisations. We had just enjoyed a holiday in Bath, and he had loved it and was interested to learn more about the life of the people who had built and lived in Aqua Sulis.

The thought of GCSE's was horrific! How would we get through this?

But after a calming cup of tea I found the number of the local private boys' school. I asked to be put through to the exam secretary.

The exam secretary was wonderful, he was so calm and straightforward, as I asked if it was possible for us to come as external candidates. I asked what exam boards the school was registered with and also what other information I needed.

This helpful gentleman explained how I needed to choose exams from the specific exam boards and then write a formal request to the headmaster. I was given all the dates to do this by. He offered me any help he could give.

Hurdle one was crossed. Why did I contact a private school? That's because I had heard from other families that they had contacted the local state schools and had not received any help. This private school had welcomed other home educating families, so that's why I called them.

Hurdle two was to research exam boards and look at courses. We couldn't do exams with a course work element, so that quickly ruled out a large proportion of the exams.

It took a few days and a lot of reading, before the exam boards were chosen. The four exam specifications were printed off, syllabuses and book lists were ready.

So far, so good. That was the easy bit. Some of the reading lists were out of date and books were out of print which was very frustrating. I was also conscious of the time pressures if we were to get ready for the beginning of the exam season in May.

Finally, I had the resources together and I looked through what we needed to learn. I then made a plan - with my son, of how much we needed to do each week to get through the courses, but also to still give us time to continue with our activities, clubs and groups.

Suddenly home education had the emphasis on the home. We needed to be there so Big son could work. But with two younger children at home we still needed to do things for their learning. It was a see saw, a balancing act to meet everyone's needs. It felt I was spinning plates while helping Big son climb through the educational hoops.

Big son had set himself a challenge and suddenly developed a hardworking, self-directed ethos. He had a plan and worked steadily through it. The way he learnt to work through those few months until the exams stayed with him. He learnt study skills and time management skills that proved invaluable at university and into life beyond education.

Steadily, Big son plodded through the course. When he didn't understand and I couldn't help, he turned to other books or looked online seeking ways to understand.

My role was not to teach as I didn't know that stuff. But I provided books, I searched for suitable websites and I encouraged this self-directed learning.

I discussed, cautiously, how he would feel if he didn't get great grades. His response, "I'm doing this three years early, and no one knows, it's like a practice run. I'm just doing my best."

Without peer pressure, he had no exam nerves. He had no expectations, so he just kept going.

The biggest problems he faced was working to time and sitting still! He also found the courses restrictive. Having always explored around a subject, he found the GCSE courses narrow. He wanted to question and explore but there wasn't time, he just had to learn the set lists of work on the syllabus.

The courses were completed by Easter and then we began to work on past papers. Mark schemes were available online, so it was easy enough to mark his work - but there was a limit to the number of past papers available. We kept being told we must be a school to access them. It was very frustrating. I attempted to write my own questions in a similar style so that he could keep practicing.

The exams were booked and paid for. We asked the school if we could visit to see the exam room. Big son's only idea of school was 'Hogwarts' from the Harry Potter films. The exam secretary agreed and showed us round. He explained the exam rules, what he could take in and showed us where the toilets were and other important things. This time was invaluable.

The day came. Big son stood outside the exam hall. He looked tiny as he waited for his name to be called, a 13 - year-old dwarfed by young men of 16. He looked so young amongst the crowd of young men sitting the exam at the same time. Definitely an emotional mummy moment.

He sat 8 papers. Then we sat back and waited for the results. He was already looking at courses for the next academic year. He decided that 4 courses was too many however 3 would be a better balance and starting in September would allow things to be better paced throughout the year. This would not just be better for him, but for us as a family.

During the summer we also looked at Open University courses. Big son enjoyed maths and sciences. He decided he would like to work on O.U. modules as they would be more in depth than GCSE's and therefore more interesting. We made no decisions at that point as we waited for the results to arrive.

A hot August morning and we were waiting at the school to be handed an envelope of results. We were ecstatic. He had passed his exams. He had B's and C's, 3 years early and self-taught. He had done it and was rightly thrilled.

At the start of the new school year someone again made a comment about how he should go to school and if he didn't, he would be unable to get any qualifications. He quietly replied, "But I already have 4 GCSE's without going to school."

Thank goodness I was never sent to school;
it would have rubbed off some of the originality.
Beatrix Potter

Chapter 8

The GCSE years were not the problem we had thought they would be. They raised many questions such as why did schools expect the students to undertake so many qualifications? Why does taking so many hold such value? Questions I could find no answer to.

GCSE's seem to be just a hoop to jump through. It's a skill to sit an exam and it seems to be more about knowing what an examiner wants, putting in a certain phrase and you get a mark, rather than an understanding of the subject.

Big son took 9 GCSE's over 3 years, plus 3 O.U. modules. He took all three sciences, yes even science can be done from home. So, armed with 30 degree points and his GCSE's, he went on to look at post 16 qualifications.

Our daughter also took a wide range of GCSE's, she too started them early. She chose different exams, working with her strengths and interests. She loved taking English literature and enjoyed reading the set books. She also sat them at the private boys' school, the only girl in a hall of boys, a splash of pink and glitter in a sea of dark uniforms. I don't know if it distracted the boys, but it didn't bother her and each year she collected more good grades.

In addition to GCSE's our daughter also attended a part-time college course. It was called Star 14 and was run one afternoon a week from 4:00 -7.30 pm. Star 14 was attended by passionate young people who really wanted to give up an evening a week to study something their schools didn't offer. In a year she achieved a BTEC level 2 in textiles and a City and Guilds qualification. It was a good introduction to formal learning, and she enjoyed it, settling into the group without a problem.

We were now looking at the post 16 world and what was needed to access it. It seemed really odd that entry criteria seemed to only ask for Maths, English and a GCSE in the subject you wanted to study at A level. Why were teenagers put under the pressure to study for so many subjects? Doing lots of GCSE's are fun for some, and I know of home educated young people who have studied for and collected 12-13 A* qualifications. Though for some, to do a few has been more beneficial.

The joy of home education has always been the way we could follow and learn through each person's interests. Even those subjects that might not have been liked could be adapted to include those interests. Our daughter does not enjoy maths, but we tried to make it relevant to her passions. She loves textiles and area of fabric, fractions of ribbon always made it seem relevant, or volume of liquid chocolate always helped!

Our daughter achieved 5 GCSE's, a BTEC level 2 with distinction and a City and Guilds certificate.

Both Big son and daughter came through secondary education with formal qualifications but also a passion to learn. They had developed a strong work ethic. Both had volunteered in the local community. Big son with the National Trust, plus one afternoon a week at a charity shop. Our daughter helped in the church creche and also did a morning a week in a different charity shop.

Both of them found Saturday jobs. These jobs taught them both a wide range of important skills. Big son worked for a gardening company and also delivered newspapers and leaflets. Our daughter worked in a fabric shop, then moved on to work in a vintage shop.

Formal qualifications to my mind are only - or should only be - a small part of a 12 - 18 year olds' education. During these six years our young people are growing and changing and should have the chance to experience as wide a range of experiences as possible.

Part time work, paid and voluntary gave them an understanding of having to be on time, presenting themselves correctly, mixing with a variety of other people as well as learning skills connected with the job, for example learning to use a till. They also had their own money and they realised the effort required to earn it, so were thoughtful about spending it.

Being home educated the growing up could be gentle. They had the opportunity to still "play" with younger children, yet also to enter the adult world in a safe and supported way. Supported by the family they reached out to new experiences and opportunities.

I'm not saying we were free from teenage moments. The children hated being referred to as teenagers, they wanted to be young adults and in the main they lived up to that term. We tried to keep the lines of communication open and no topic was barred. We talked honestly about drink, drugs and relationships.

We stuck to our routine of getting up and starting 'school' work as we always had done, as we felt this was an important discipline. But we continued to work with their interests. The desire to do exams came from them and there was little reluctance to complete work. Our working day was balanced, with breaks when needed and times to do nothing, so that we never had times of overwhelming exam pressure.

Armed with GCSE's and the invaluable skills for life, transferable skills from the part time jobs, Big son also had 30 degree points from O.U. and a BTEC level 3 in Business, so he applied for university.

Big son was accepted into university and headed off. His skills for life were the most important thing he took with him. He had studied like a university student for years and knew how to organise his time, plan and research his work. Budgeting and cooking skills meant he lived within his means and he had skills to resolve problems constructively. Skills for life learnt from life.

Our daughter entered the local further education college at 15 and did a BTEC level 3 in fashion. She entered the university of her choice at 17, a year early. She too found that the life skills were the most important part of her education. She cooked from scratch to keep within budget. She also used her sewing skills to help her fellow students and used these skills to gain some ad hoc work for a jewellery designer.

Notice the difference:
A child's disability is the focus of traditional classroom settings, but his abilities are the focus of the home environment.

Sandra K. Cook

Everybody is a genius.
But if you judge a fish
By its ability to climb a tree,
It will spend its whole life believing
It is stupid.

Albert Einstein

Chapter 9

Yes, but… as with all education, it has to fit the person. Having read this account you might be thinking that our home education has been easy. Follow that style and all will be well. Nah, it is always about the person, not the formula.

We have had our ups and downs. There were days when no one wanted to do anything. When Mum was grumpy and couldn't explain something the way the recipient could understand. The day when school a million miles away seemed a great option!

It's better not to ask why the stencil of Britain is missing the tip of Cornwall, everyone can have days that are not good.

Those days happen, put the kettle on, go for a walk and take a breath. Quietly think why things went wrong; tiredness, illness, or something else? Look and listen and try to find a different approach.

Our daughter desperately wanted to read. She tried and tried, but it wasn't happening for her. She couldn't recognise the difference between a capital A and H.

We then found out that she was dyslexic and had such bad eyesight with astigmatism. So, we kept reading to her. We made letters from playdough and sandpaper, reinforced spelling with touch and not sight. She might not be able to read but we made sure that we focused on what she could do. She could use a sewing machine. She could focus on the machine foot and move the fabric into her field of vision, she didn't need to use scanning vision. At age 5 she was making simple skirts for herself. It gave her confidence. She could do something special, something many adults admitted to not being able to do.

Finally, we got a prescription that was correct, our non-reader went to a reader in literally 5 minutes. She was fitted with her new glasses and we walked round to the Building Society.

Standing there she suddenly announced, "Mummy you must ask about mortgages."

I stood opened mouthed. "Why?"

"Cause the sign says, 'Ask about our mortgages'."

This from the child who would struggle to read her name earlier. We hadn't worried about the problem of learning to read, just found what she could do and thrive at, while plodding on working at the basic skills.

We also had Little son, the only one of the family to have been born this century. He proved again and again that what would work with the other two wouldn't work with him. He loved the routine of "schoolwork time" but for him everything was to be a struggle. He needed a different and individual approach.

Sitting still to listen to a story or instruction was a nightmare, but by allowing him to draw or build blocks quietly, this gave me time to read to the others, although he was listening too. He would talk about what we had read. He was listening and learning, even if he didn't appear to be. Slowly it evolved until he would sit and listen to a story or a film. In fact, he reached a stage where he sat still and silently so as not to miss any of the story.

Little son was always an active character who really needed to understand the why of doing something. It had to be relevant. Measuring wood and angles to make a stool would keep he was happy, as it made sense. Measuring angles on a maths paper – why?

Despite his love of stories and vast vocabulary, he could describe things well, but when asked to write a story, that blank page scare him and he fought a battle. Why write when you can only retell a story, which had already been written brilliantly by the author.

As my father had said when Little son was a toddler, "That one's wired differently."

He is different. He learns when he understands a purpose. We had an allotment and talked about cell walls, turgid pressure, osmosis, etc while watering and in response to him noticing wilting plants. Things always had to be firmly rooted in reality, learning from a page made no sense to him.

Home education had become a much larger community than when we had started out. This had advantages for Little son. Hundreds of families had created different groups and through these we had access to some amazing workshops, classes and activities. But he didn't seem to access them, due to the noise, busyness and speed of delivery, leaving him lost and bewildered.

Many times, I thought seriously about school; but seeing his 'lostness' in group learning I knew he would not cope.

At age 12 I knew it was time to see if he had any learning difficulties.

It took nearly two years from asking the GP for a referral. The psychologist confirmed what I'd known but hadn't felt like acknowledging: he was diagnosed with dyslexia and autistic spectrum disorder.

As I'd sat and thought at the beginning of this journey – "I'm no teacher.", " Can I do this?", these questions came back and were added by – "I'm no special needs teacher" , "Can I really do this?"

The ease of access through the internet now made the research for information so much easier than those first days of trying to find out about home education last century. I read up all I could about Autism and learning disabilities. I researched special schools and read their curriculum. The more I read the more it was confirmed, I knew my son best. The psychologist had mentioned that because I had adapted to his needs, I had helped mask many symptoms of his autism and needs. I had given him skills that he needed to cope. By teaching him by example he was learning social skills, by teaching him 1:1 he was accessing the academic skills he needed.

This time made me think, really think, again and again about what education is for. Why do we place certain skills over others? Why is the curriculum what it is?

My daughter asked me this thought-provoking question: "Why are some subjects deemed greater than others? If you are useless at maths or English, then everyone says you're stupid. But if you are useless at music or art then everyone says never mind, you're not musical or artistic. Why can't we accept what people can do, not what they can't?"

So then how could we go on and meet Little son's needs?

Our priority had to be to build skills for independent living and build his confidence.

"How?"

The three main areas we looked at first were the life skills of buying things, to meet need and handle money. To use public transport, to be able to navigate his way around. Then to encourage communication skills and decision making.

Then we looked at what he loved to do. He had a passion for working with wood, so we found a woodturning group that met monthly and a woodcarving group that met each week that he was allowed to join. I had to attend with him - this was a requirement of health and safety, but also, he needed my support.

These groups were primarily made up of older, mainly retired gentlemen, who accepted him and generously shared their knowledge with him. Little son's woodworking knowledge and skills grew, but also so did his social skills. Slowly he left my side and began to take part in some conversation, if they were about the projects that he was working on.

We also went out and about and took part in some voluntary work with the wildlife trust. Coppicing trees in the woodland and feeding sticks into the fire was a fantastic day out.

With this newfound passion and skills, we talked about how to use them in a way to earn a living. He said he'd like to be a furniture maker or a forester. My job was to research how he could do that and find out about possible courses.

Little son knew that to go to college to do what he wanted, he would need to meet the entry criteria. They were asking for Maths, English and a science GCSE. He faced up to his learning disabilities and began the torturous uphill struggle to take these subjects.

Biology learning was fine. It seemed straightforward, black and white. It was a subject he could see. It made sense until we looked at past papers and although he could name and label, so many other questions were hidden in English he struggled to understand. Frequently, our learning time disintegrated as he stared at words saying it all made no sense.

English was an on-going nightmare, his reading was ok, as long as the environment was quiet. But if he needed to invent stories it was a hurdle to keep practicing. The hardest thing was comprehension questions that asked him to consider the characters' feelings, or discuss what the author might have been thinking, or ask him how he would react if he was in the characters' situation. He would just look blank; this style of question was beyond him.

Slowly, very slowly we plodded down the exam specification. We talked through answers, on days when thinking and writing would have been too much. Reading and writing for him gave him space to think through these difficult concepts.

The discipline of years of sitting down together in the mornings had paid off. The routine helped keep us going. Dangling the carrot of spending time doing woodwork or a trip to the cinema, or a woodland walk helped us get through the school work time and helped remind us that this wasn't going to last for ever.

Maths wasn't much easier. Again, it was the way questions were worded, maths hidden in language. The confusion of negative numbers, where the bigger the number the smaller it is, struggle, struggle, struggle. Constant small steps. Revisiting and revising before moving on.

In all subjects we constantly tried to set work in reality. To work on budgets and food bills, we worked with money. To work out the area of a room to buy carpet all made maths relevant and therefore a subject worth learning. Though I did struggle to find how we could use algebra and equations in life…though I suppose a mathematician reading this would disagree.

In the January before the GCSE's we chose to drop biology and concentrate on maths and English. The course he was interested in asked for only those two subjects, along with a passion for working to high standards with wood.

After school work time each day we continued to learn from life. A biology concept we could talk about while gardening or cooking. The pressure of writing and spelling removed allowed us to talk and explore and grasp concepts in a non-threatening way.

When the stress or hypersensitivity of autism took over, we could walk away, and do something else, make toast, ride a bike, chill out and listen to music. Sitting on a hilltop on a windy morning, maybe we would manage to create a story together without that threatening piece of white paper stretched out before us.

Luckily for us at this time a company set up in Coventry called Tutors and exams, through them families could access any exam, any exam board and sit the exams. They had a wonderful can do, no problem, let's do it, attitude. They helped us access past papers. They arranged for us to have "Form 8" (document to prove additional educational need) done to allow Little son more time for sitting exams.

We were able to visit the centre, see the private room where he would sit his exams. He would sit his exams alone and he was introduced to his invigilator. No shocks, no surprises, no extra fears. The building even had a coffee shop so I could stay on site and he knew exactly where I would be, no extra concerns.

But what of the future? There was a need and support was going to be required if he went on to do a college course. So, I began to ask and I phoned department after department seeking support for him.

Twice I was told the only way to access the support needed was to put him in school. Huh! Why?

Why would I put a young person in school environment who needs to wear ear defenders, sunglasses and a hood if he goes out, into a school where these wouldn't be allowed? It would be an environment that would be alien, challenging and noisy, full of unpredictable teenagers. If he struggled 1:1 with a tutor or me helping him, then how would he cope and learn in a busy classroom?

No. I would not do it! There must be a way to continue in our own environment, where we could nurture his needs and build on his skills and support his confidence without sending him to school.

We looked into EHCP's (Educational Health and Social Care Plans).

We looked at CAF's (Common Assessment Frameworks).

Armed with the autism diagnosis and the determination to find a great outcome for our son's future, we phoned, emailed, asked questions and then did it all over again. Department after department, calling out of order numbers and being put on hold as I tried to find the help we needed.

Autism and exam stress was not a good combination, they didn't mix! When it got too bad, we would put down the books and go out for a walk, or go off to do some kayaking. Mental health, self-confidence and security were more important than results.

When were you last asked your GCSE results? They are only hoops to jump through.

Let's remove the hoops.

The government attempts to raise standards and make everyone continue studying maths and English until age 18. For those who struggle this becomes a huge barrier. Some just need to spend time working on vocational skills which will provide them with work. Funding streams are tied to these subjects and for our son this was a huge hurdle.

But we were experienced home educators by now and we knew if we couldn't find him the course that would meet his needs, we would work from home and find those who could help him develop his skills. We needed a course without the mill stone of GCSE's.

The most important thing is mental health, it is so easily damaged, not so easily restored. It is hidden and fragile. After 15 years of nurture we were not prepared to have it destroyed.

Ask, seek, ask, seek, whilst holding onto the knowledge that you know your child's needs. Don't let the system destroy or belittle, we all have skills, and our children will develop despite the system.

We finally found the right department and they agreed to work on an EHCP without going to school. We received the document and support from the educational psychologist, agreeing that he could be exempt from exams and concentrate on a furniture making course and that a 1:1 support worker would be provided to help him.

It doesn't matter how slowly you go
as long as you do not stop.

Confucius

Chapter 10

Stuff!

I wasn't sure where to put this chapter. But I was sure that I needed to put it in. For a while I was a local contact for Educational Otherwise. Families would phone and want to talk about the possibility of removing their children from school. After we had talked about socialization, how to de-register, and maybe exams, then I'd be asked what stuff would be needed and if the cost would be prohibitive.

There is no definitive list as to what you need to home educate. Visit a school and look in any educational catalogue and it's easy to be sucked into the idea that a perfect education requires a lot of 'stuff', specialist equipment and rooms dedicated to separate topics.

When we began to home educate, we didn't even have a home computer, but that was last century. We started our education within our home. Most families will have everything they need in their home to educate their children. A kitchen can provide a rich learning environment, not just for cooking, but for maths and chemistry. Measuring jugs, scales and ingredients as well as all the packaging and labelling can be used to learn.

We once did a project, reading the labels of ingredients in the kitchen and then marking on a map and seeing where all our food came from. This led to talk of air miles, pollution and cost.

We mixed oil and water, salt or sugar, and had solutions to discover. We left these on a saucer and watched what happened over a few days.

Packaging can provide cardboard for crafts and plastic trays make great trays to lay out science experiments. Think Blue Peter and suddenly everything has a new use.

Lego and wooden blocks can be used for their original purpose, but also make great maths counting blocks. Board games, craft materials and the rest of the stuff, the stuff that most children's bedrooms are cluttered with are all great starting points for learning.

Look about your house - a tape measure, sewing machine, the contents of the garden shed, a packet of seeds and a pot and you've got all the educational materials you need. Most of us have a wealth of educational materials if we just spend a moment and look.

We did buy a few things, some magnets and a magnifying glass. We were given a basic microscope and bought from the Works; a plastic jaw, heart and skeleton. It wasn't a huge outlay, especially as they were used so often.

Life has changed with the advent of the internet, home computers and google. There is so much information, work sheets, activities and games all available at the click of a button. Instant access to GCSE specifications and past papers. There are free courses as well as Open University courses all available online. The Covid 19 pandemic has increased the amount of online education material that is now available.

Each family will choose how much they want to use the digital world and how much they want to physically do, but it is useful to join in and watch, for example, an expert explaining about the planets and space exploration. It is also useful to see contradictory accounts and debate these.

Learning can happen everywhere and at any time or place. The clocks in your house, the money in your purse, the meal on your table and most of all the people you meet are all learning opportunities.

There may not be box ticking paper evidence of what your children have learnt. That doesn't matter. Your children have learnt the needed skills. Sometimes it's hard not to be blinded by how schools do things and assess learning.

Other children may wave a certificate at your family and your heart sinks as your children haven't done that. But by keeping a diary I can look back and reassure myself that my children certainly gained a wide variety of learning opportunities.

As I've mentioned we have even done GCSE's from home, including all three of the sciences. Chemistry and physics, yes, we did the practical work from home. We used Nanna's gas cooker instead of a Bunsen burner for experiments, until we bought a camping stove to use to heat beakers (jam jars) of liquid.

More important than all the stuff has been people. We went into the nearest city to join in Chinese New Year and watched the dragon dance. Then to the Chinese restaurant and asked our waitress to teach us how to say 'please and thank you' in Mandarin Chinese.

An elderly neighbour played the trumpet and gave us some ad hoc lessons. A neighbour across the road was Italian. She gave us pasta making lessons and an introduction to the language.

My mother had taught science in school and came over one day with a cow's heart and lungs, which the butcher had happily given her. She was surrounded by 5 children of different ages who watched fascinated as she dissected them and told them about keeping their hearts healthy. Two hours disappeared so fast as they watched, listened and asked questions.

So many wonderful people, too many to list here, as they would fill this book. But they willingly share their skills and expertise with us. They excited us with their passion for their interest and hobbies. There was also a wealth of unnamed people who we watched, changing a car tyre or hanging a poster from a hoarding. There were the men from Severn Trent water who let us listen to the water of an underground leak and the tradesmen who took time to show interested children what they were doing and how things worked. I would love to thank them all, they extended our world, our learning, our knowledge and enriched our learning experiences.

Home education isn't about the acquisition of stuff. Though I must admit I do have an addiction to books! I can't resist a second-hand book sale or a car boot sale. I struggle to buy a book on its own (it might get lonely) and a trip to a National Trust property has to include a look around the second-hand book shop so that I can rehome the books. Books have been a window into a wider world.

A bit of imagination, creativity, the world we live in, conversation and exploration and you have everything you need to create a learning experience that is unique and without walls.

Stuff is not the main thing to introduce your child to a life of learning. Take a moment to stop and look, think outside the box and you start to see the potential of everything. Don't worry about stuff.

Tell me and I forget.
Teach me and I remember,
Involve me and I learn.

Benjamin Franklin

Chapter 11

Think back to your own school days… what do you remember from it?

Can you remember every law of physics? Every French verb? Can you remember which 'bits' of history you were taught?

I expect the answer is no, you can't, you were taught but didn't remember. You take through life what information you need or were passionately interested in. Therefore, I don't think a home educating parent needs to worry about telling their child everything on the curriculum.

From my observations I have seen that a person learns mainly from what they do and see, rather than what they are told. Damming a stream on a beach and noticing the rise in water levels, the silting up of the bend in their newly dug channel had far more of an impact than a geography lesson.

"But… there will be gaps…"

When this was said to me, I think I must have looked blank, because I know my own education had gaps. Bits were missed because of illness or having to share a book and not getting the chance to reread a section I didn't understand, or even just forgetting.

Gaps, I don't think so. If you want to know something, then you'll find it out. Know how to research and you can fill any gaps that you feel you have. To my mind the most important thing is the ability to find out and learn when you need the information.

When it comes to exams, yes you need the specification of what you need to know. It is interesting to know that the specifications for different exam boards can be very different. Yet all of the students can say they have a qualification in the subject. This brings us back to the question of gaps. Do students of different exam boards think the others have gaps because they know different things? No, they just know they both have the same qualification, but know different areas.

Gaps? I think it can be summed up as, just different knowledge. Think how often you hear on a quiz show a contestant saying 'if I'd had the other set of questions the outcome would have been different.' Different knowledge, different life experiences, not gaps.

In a country that is very diverse in ethnicity and where we embrace other ways of life and religious differences, why then are we so narrowly focused on a one size fits all education? Let's embrace diversity of learning styles and interests and knowledge.

I very much wanted my children to be exposed to as wide a variety of experiences as possible. I think I had a fear of one of them having a talent and me failing to see it. To overcome this, I made sure we went to a huge range of different places.

Once a month on a Thursday lunchtime the local university put on a free concert, for just about 30 minutes. It was ideal for a family of young children. Each month featured different instruments and groups. It didn't for us inspire a musical genius, more an interest in science, as to how each instrument made its sound.

When I look back and re-read some of the scrap books we made, I'm amazed at how much we did, the variety of places we went. I tried to include the children in planning these trips. Then they had a knowledge of what they might see and something to look out for, so they were ready to take in details of the visit. Preparation sparked questions and they were ready to receive the answer.

I firmly believe if you ask a question you want an answer. Then you are more likely to retain the answer. Being told stuff you're not ready to receive or are not interested in then means you are more likely forget the information.

Being at home, the children were not confined, and they saw problems that needed solving. Problem solving was not a planned lesson, we just got on with finding a solution, so that nothing was a sterile isolated lesson. The power fused, the sink was blocked, the car tyre went flat, the road we usually used was shut - all the everyday challenges that needed to be sorted. Problem solving is a major life skill which we all use, and home education helped us develop that resilience and skill.

The other thing we noticed was that because adults were available, we were not a separate species. We were sharers in what the children were doing. Our reactions to events and activities and how we reacted to problems was observed by the children. They didn't just have the reactions of peers and the peer power struggles of being in the classroom.

The biggest tool in our home education box has been to listen, to be available to the children, to answer questions. Also, to admit to not having knowledge and being seen to research an answer helped the children to see that it was good to research and how they could do it.

My job has been, not teacher, but to provide learning experiences, to support their questions and help them find out their answers. Sometimes it is interesting to see how many areas of the curriculum can be covered in a few hours. For example, one lunchtime we went to listen to a talk at the local museum:

Checked route on map. (Geography)
Read bus timetables. (Maths)
Read poster on bus about using a tissue when sneezing, then bin the tissue and wash hands. Discussed the advertising campaign. (Biology and English)
Attended the museum talk. (History and social skills)
Estimating whether there was enough money left from the bus trip to have a drink, or whether to spend it on a box of ice-cream to enjoy over the weekend. (Financial education)

You get the picture, there is so much going on all day.

In the early years, there was so much on offer in the way of clubs, activities and special interest groups. The library ran summer holiday reading schemes for the under 11's and we read through the summers. Local churches held holiday clubs and the nature reserve held walks and talks.

After the age of eleven, it grew more difficult to find appropriate activities, but they were there. It just took a little more looking.

We found in the back of a university prospectus, a maths class for 14-year olds, held once a month at our local university. We also discovered that Imperial college London offered a science week summer school. The Smallpeice Trust also offered summer courses. Big son spent a week living in University, working with others passionate about maths and science.

We would look at local adverts and posters and then if it looked interesting, we would contact the group. In most cases the children were welcome to attend the talks and events. Sometimes a group would ask if an adult attend with the child, no problem. Only once were we told no children were allowed.

Ask questions, talk to people, it's all part of the rich experience of learning.

How could I home educate? Well it wasn't just me; it was the children. They were interested and inquisitive. All I did was provide those experiences.

Would I do it again? Oh yes.

It has been fun. I've been taught so much. It's been a pleasure to watch the children grow and mature and develop into the adults they are today.

At times it might have felt as if I was spinning plates. Some of it felt as if I had to just help them through hoops. But it has been an amazing experience. Thank you all three of you for the "school" years that we have shared.

Thank you to everyone who was involved in our incredible journey.

Chapter 12

The Covid pandemic has changed the perception of home education. All parents have suddenly and in most cases, not wanted to become responsible for their children's education. They haven't had the luxury of time to think about becoming a home educator.

Hopefully, as many have tasted the joys and struggles of home education, there will now be a greater respect of parents who choose to follow this path.

We live in a culture that has devalued motherhood and parental responsibility. Schools have taken over the responsibility of academic, social and moral education of most children. What home educating parents did, was not understood by a lot of people, both men and women.

In our society we seem to be defined by our work. This is often the first question asked at a party or a meeting with new people. They raise an eyebrow,
"Oh, you don't work. You just look after the children?"

The impression is that we just sit about and watch daytime T.V. while drinking coffee.

To all of you parents who decided to "just" home educate, I salute you. Well done for taking on the most complex, involved and time consuming, but undervalued job on the planet.

However you became a home educating parent, whatever the reason behind your family's decision, to all of you who spin a thousand plates and help your children through life's hoops, congratulations - you are amazing.

www.ingramcontent.com/pod-product-compliance
Lightning Source LLC
Chambersburg PA
CBHW052358060726

47592CB00019B/1530